SHUTTER SPEED 2

Lily
Publications

Published by Lily Publications Ltd, PO Box 33, Ramsey, Isle of Man, British Isles, IM99 4LP
Tel: +44 (0) 1624 898446   Fax: +44 (0) 1624 898449   www.lilypublications.co.uk

INTRODUCTION

The first Shutterspeed collection of Dave Collister's TT racing photography was published four years ago. Packed with exceptional images spanning the three decades up to 2010, it was a sell-out. With such demand for atmospheric action photographs with Collister's keen eye for detail, a sequel just had to be published.

Here in *Shutterspeed 2*, on a similar theme but with a different approach, Collister has selected his own favourite TT shots taken since 2010. As with the first book, he has been assisted with text editing by motorcycle journalist and regular Lily Publications author Mick Duckworth.

In addition to recent Mountain Course TT racing, Shutterspeed 2 also includes images from the Southern 100, the friendly grass-roots meeting held on the Isle of Man's 4.25-mile Billown circuit in July.

Dave Collister, who sees conversation with the riders he photographs as a key part of his work, is grateful to the stars of the show who gave time to comment on his shots, helping to enrich the content of captions.

Finally the authors and publisher would like thank the following for their help with this publication; Gaz Aldridge (Gaztec), John Hogan of 'Superbike' magazine, Chippy Wood, Christine Collister and all the riders of the TT and Southern 100 who have helped to make ths book possible.

Miles Cowsill
Lily Publications, Isle of Man
November 2014

An iconic Mountain Course location, Kate's Cottage. Spectators watch Keith Amor plummet down the hill towards Creg-ny-Baa in a 2011 Supersport race.

THE WORLD'S GREATEST ROAD RACE

The incomparable Isle of Man TT stands apart from any other motorcycle race and, indeed, any other event in the realm of motor sport. Awesome to watch, TT racing over the Mountain Circuit on machines capable of 200mph is an exacting test of rider and machine, fraught with a level of danger to participants shared by few other legal activities.

In a typical major motorcycle race, 20 or so competitors vie with each other for about 40 minutes on a purpose-built track with a two- or three-mile lap. All of the turns have run-off areas with gravel traps or tyre walls to soften the landings of any riders who fall down or ride off the track. Spectators are kept at a safe distance, sometimes quite remote from the action.

In the TT, a race grid may have 80 or more starters and a single lap is over 37.73 miles of public highway temporarily closed off for racing. The roads, mostly as wide as a typical single-carriageway rural route, are bordered by kerbs, stone walls, iron gates, lampposts and other solid objects, along with houses and other permanent structures. Extensive efforts are made to cushion the most obvious dangers with foam or air-bags, but only a few of the sharper corners on road junctions have any emergency run-off provision. There are places where spectators can be incredibly close to the action, offering a unique and sometimes terrifying experience that just can't be matched at a typical circuit.

A major aspect of the TT that sets it apart is that riders don't all set off at once, but are flagged away from the start line at 10-second intervals. Positions during and at the end of the race are calculated by correcting for individual riders' elapsed times. Rarely confusing for spectators, the time trial nature of the racing tends to add interest, while close-quarters' dicing between two or more riders does

occurs. The official race timing is electronic, with each machine carrying a transponder, also useful for recording times over individual sections of the lap and clocking speeds on the long, but far from smooth, mile-long Sulby Straight.

The Mountain Circuit is estimated to incorporate at least 220 bends, some gentle enough to be straight-lined and a couple sharp enough to be taken at less than 30mph. It has been estimated that on some machines 225 gearchanges are made in a single lap. The road climbs to 427m (1400ft) above sea level on the Mountain section and although Manx highway engineers endeavour to maintain the surface in prime condition, it tends to settle back to the undulations of old, especially where it skirts the swampy Curragh from Ballaugh to Sulby. The many crests and countless bumps throw the fastest bikes into alarming, barely-controllable wheelies and wiggles, so chassis preparation and suspension fine-tuning is as important as engine power and reliability for success.

Sidecar racing, now rarely seen at the grands prix, offers variety and is popular with spectators. The drivers and passengers of the jinking and slewing low-slung outfits are only inches off the road and their engines worked almost to destruction, being revved flat-out for long periods.

Photography covering big international races tends to crop in very close on riders. The surroundings are rarely of interest and huge deserted stands built for Formula One or NASCAR crowds can be an embarrassment. But as Dave Collister's work makes so clear, the Isle of Man TT offers a much bigger picture.

In the period during which the TT photos in this book were taken, there were five solo races in the programme and two for sidecars. The Superbike race is for machines

How timing was done before it went fully digital. One of the timekeepers' old pairs of analogue clocks at the start line.

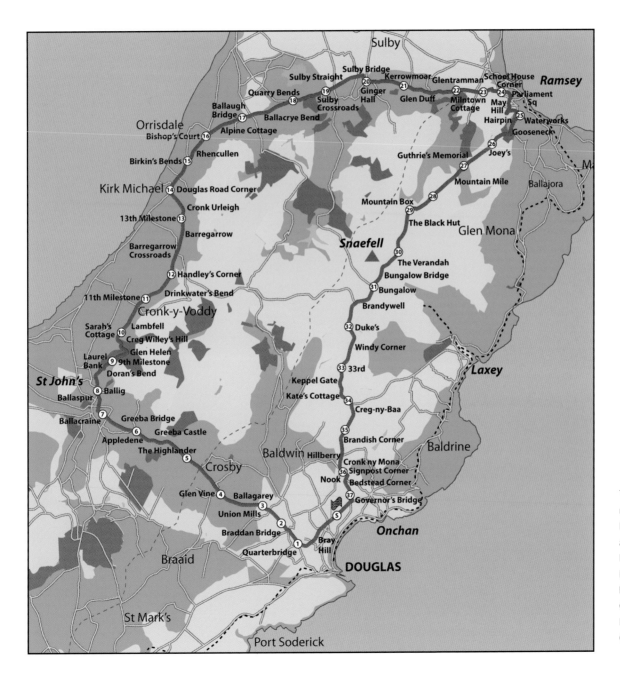

Sulby

Ramsey

School House
Corner
Sulby Bridge
Kerrowmoar
Glentramman
Sulby Straight
Ginger
Hall
Parliament
Sq
Quarry Bends
Glen Duff
Milntown
Cottage
Sulby
Crossroads
May
Hill
Ballaugh
Bridge
Ballacrye Bend
Hairpin
Orrisdale
Waterworks
Alpine Cottage
Bishop's Court
Gooseneck
Rhencullen
Joey's
Guthrie's Memorial
Birkin's Bends
Mountain Mile
Ballajora
Kirk Michael
Douglas Road Corner
Cronk Urleigh
Mountain Box
13th Milestone
The Black Hut
Glen Mona
Barregarrow
Snaefell
Barregarrow
Crossroads
The Verandah
Handley's Corner
Bungalow Bridge
Drinkwater's Bend
Bungalow
11th Milestone
Brandywell
Cronk-y-Voddy
Sarah's
Cottage
Lambfell
Duke's
Creg Willey's Hill
Glen Helen
Windy Corner
Laurel
Bank
9th Milestone
Doran's Bend
33rd
Laxey
St John's
Keppel Gate
Ballig
Kate's Cottage
Ballaspur
Creg-ny-Baa
Ballacraine
Greeba Bridge
Brandish Corner
Greeba Castle
Baldrine
Appledene
The Highlander
Baldwin
Hillberry
Crosby
Cronk ny Mona
Signpost Corner
Nook
Bedstead Corner
Glen Vine
Ballagarey
Governor's Bridge
Union Mills
Bray
Hill
Onchan
Braddan Bridge
Quarterbridge
DOUGLAS
Braaid
St Mark's
Port Soderick

Two corners acquired
new names in 2013:
Molyneux's on the
approach to the 11th
Milestone and
McGuinness's
between Handley's
Corner and
Barregarrow
Crossroads

It's easy to see why this bumpy section near Glentramman, known as 'Conker Fields', attracts spectators and photographers. The rider is James Hillier, in practice for the 2013 TT on his Kawasaki.

conforming to an international Superbike formula. Engines can be of up to 1000cc with or three or four cylinders, or 1200c with two. The Superstock race is for approved production models on road-legal tyres (not slicks) with capacity limits as for Superbike. The Supersport 1 and 2 is for production machines with approved modifications. Engines can be of up to 600cc with four cylinders, 675cc with three and 750cc with two. The premier Senior TT is

open to Superbike and Superstock machines, plus others admitted at the discretion of the organisers. The Lightweight race, run since 2012 is for production-based machines of up to 650cc with twin-cylinder engines. Sidecars conform to international Formula 2 rules, with 600cc front-mounted engines. TT Zero is for zero-emissions motorcycles, which in practice means electric-powered prototypes.

When the original Shutterspeed book came out in 2010, the Isle of Man TT races had come through a period of major change. Only a few years earlier, some paddock gossips had been suggesting that the TT would reach it's 100th birthday in 2007 and be wound down. It would be for the best, as the golden days of public roads racing were long gone, Mountain Course racing was an anachronism that looked out of place beside modern circuit racing, while fewer and fewer riders were willing to take on the difficult and hazardous Mountain Course.

Yet, far from dying out, the TT has continued to evolve and has bounced back from obscurity. Staging a successful Centenary was only the start of further change. Staking its claim as one of the world's major motorcycling festivals, the TT's profile has been raised far and wide by the success of the 2011 documentary film Closer to the Edge shot in 3D along with pan-global transmission of high-quality race-by-race TV coverage.

Young riders with an aptitude for road racing have been actively encouraged to join in, 'holiday racers' not up to the pace are no longer welcome and the whole operation is more professional. Perhaps inevitably the TT is also becoming more commercialised, although it is still a world apart from the highly corporate MotoGP scene.

Reaching beyond the traditional hardcore motorcycle enthusiast, the TT is justifiably coming to be regarded as a 'must see' sporting experience, alongside other great traditional events, like the Monaco Formula One GP, the Le Mans 24 Hours race or the Tour de France. Watching finely skilled and extremely brave riders master the Mountain Course at speeds that would have been dismissed as imposssible not so long ago is an unforgettable experience.

Chippy Wood, a hardened professional racing photographer who has unrivalled experience of MotoGPs and British Superbike was working at the 2014 TT after 12 years away. Following the Superbike race I asked him what he thought.

"Absolutely incredible! I was just blown away by the speed and the skill of the riders," he said. "That's the most exciting motorcycle photography I've done in years."

The best riders are lapping at a breathtaking 130mph-plus on Superbikes and even Superstock machines restricted to near-standard specification and road tyres are up there now. Machine development and the easing of a couple of corners primarily to improve day-to-day road safety on the Island have helped, but is also down to the riders. TT riders apply all their skill and intelligence in the quest to complete a perfect lap of the 37.73-mile Course. It's a challenge: when I was preparing this book, John McGuinness told me that he went to the Centenary TT of 2007 with the aim of hoisting the lap record to 130mph, a major milestone for the record books. He wanted to do it unofficially in practice to get people talking. He tried hard but failed. It was only in the final race of the meeting, the Senior, that he achieved his goal – and before anyone else.

I also consulted Cameron Donald, winner of both the Superbike and Superstock races in 2008, who said that technical improvements to the machinery push the rider on.

"This is why the TT lap records are always being broken, both bikes and riders continue to improve," he told me. "As a racer wanting to win you ride the bike until you're on the edge, if the bike is working well you will be lapping at a higher speed before you reach the edge."

I think it's a similar situation in photography, which has, like the TT, been changing a lot. Even 10 years ago,

FASTER RACING, BETTER CAMERAS

You never know when it's going to happen. Jonathan Howarth's fall on Bray Hill seconds after he started the 2013 Senior race, which he escaped from with minor injuries, but several spectators were injured, some seriously.

Collister gets down to it. Taken at Ballaugh by Spanish photographer Pedro Mordt.

be seen on a banner in the background, or a particular sticker on a bike's fairing may have to be clearly identifiable. I'm not knocking the hard-working photographers who shoot this stuff but it conflicts with the principles of what I set out to achieve from a practice or race session.

One of my worst experiences was during the 2007 Centenary TT practice week, when I agreed to produce a series of 'then and now' shots for a magazine. It was a miserable time knowing exactly where I'd be the next evening, slavishly copying another photographer's angle from 50 years before.

For me it's always a matter of quality over quantity. I shoot where I want, capturing my own vision of what the TT means to me. Ironically, I have steadily built up a good number of magazine and other outlets that appreciate this approach.

Wearing a photographer's pass lets you go where the general public can't, but carries responsibility. You mustn't do anything to create a hazard, either to the riders or yourself. At today's speeds, spectators can be just as vulnerable as photographers and I was unfortunate enough to witness Jonathan Howarth falling off on Bray Hill in the 2013 Senior race. When his bike broke into flying bits, in the immediate aftermath I feared at least one motionless spectator had been killed. In the event, several were injured but thankfully there were no fatalities.

That episode reinforced my belief that it's not just accredited photographers who put themselves in the potential firing line. Everyone needs to keep their wits about them, always thinking what they would do in a crash situation, because when it happens you have to react in a split-second.

Not being a full-time professional photographer has

no-one foresaw the drastic improvements in digital camera sensor technology. The image quality of the finest-grain transparency slide film of old, once the gold standard, has now been surpassed. Incredible performance even high up the ISO scale, once a taboo area because of graininess (or 'noise') means we can now use super-fast shutter speeds to freeze the quickest action, even in low light conditions. The biggest limiting factor is not the camera but a photographer's own imagination.

I have never been interested in shooting the TT for a photo agency. In that situation you are expected to get maximum coverage of a six-lap race by taking most of your shots from 'safe bet' locations. Your chances of getting the most striking and original images, which carry a high risk of not working, are much reduced.

Commissioned photos may require a sponsors' name to

good and bad points. Not shooting bikes solidly all year means I never feel stale or burned out come June, so I can unleash that stored-up creative energy like a coiled spring. On the down side, it can be a pain juggling a day job with last-minute requests for press or commercial shoots that can make me pretty unpopular at work.

I only once absolutely had to turn a photo job down. It was a biggie: James May with his Toy Stories Meccano bike and sidecar for a Radio Times front cover. But being asked to do another front page job was a massive honour: shooting the cover image for the 2012 TT official programme. Saying 'yes' immediately, I then endured three weeks of worry and sleep deprivation. It was to be an unprecedented three-hour shoot, featuring John McGuinness on a Honda Fireblade Superbike, plus Dave Molyneux and his passenger Patrick Farrance on Moly's freshly painted DMR Kawasaki Sidecar. That's 33 TT wins in one photo. To make it possible, a Mountain Road closing order was enforced from Ramsey Hairpin to The Bungalow.

The plan was for an image that looked nothing like one normally taken during a TT practice or race. My idea was to make it a tracking shot from a moving car using two cameras and car-mounted strobe flashes to give it an unusual studio feel.

The worrying bit was the weather forecast for the scheduled April morning. The island had basked in spring sunshine for a whole fortnight. Surely it could hold that way for a few more days?

It didn't. When I drove over the Mountain at 8am, the rain was lashing down. Oh yeah, this was going to look like no other TT shot alright!

Poor Paul Phillips, the Island's director of motor sport and ultimately in charge, looked very anxious when I

found him waiting at Ramsey Hairpin. To make matters worse, John's Honda TT Legends Superbike had slick tyres fitted. There were no spare wheels for treaded intermediates: I could see the newspaper headlines already.

Then, as it often can on the Island, the rain suddenly stopped and the cloud started to lift. The road was still soaking wet but at least the photos wouldn't show sheets of rain and standing water.

The weather gradually brightened and improved, throwing up magnificent grey clouds in a stormy blue sky. We managed to get some good results in the limited time we had before the road re-opened. In fact they probably turned out better than if we had been blessed with fine weather. Bright sunlight, with heavy shadows, is not always ideal for the best photography.

A bonus was being able to use one of the on-bike

Fiftieth anniversary re-enactment of a photo taken of the Honda team on its historic TT debut in 1959. The 2009 team is (from left) Nick Crowe, his passenger Mark Cox, Neil Tuxworth of Honda Racing , John McGuinness, Steve Plater, Guy Martin, team manager Havier Beltran and senior technician Julian Boland.

camera rigs hand-made by extreme on-board cam specialist Gaz Aldridge, which was fitted to the front of McGuinness's Fireblade. We had just enough time to get one run up the Mountain as fast as John felt comfortable with cold slick tyres on a damp road.

Desperate to get a result in the time we had, I actually said "can you look like your really trying, please John?" to receive a withering reply from the then outright lap record holder: "I always ride the same way, everywhere." The result of that hasty run is the shot on the cover of this book.

On the following pages my selection of TT and Southern 100 images is accompanied by my comments on each shot, and in many cases, some 'behind the visor' insight is provided by the rider or sidecar driver involved.

Left: I think this 'as the Crow flies' shot commissioned for the 2008 official TT programme summed up Nick Crowe's team: serious about winning but also enjoying a good laugh. Nick was suspended from a hoist, while sponsor Andy Faragher and passenger Mark Cox ham it up. A graphic designer added cartoon crows to my image, criticised by some as too cheesy.

Right: Magazine shoot for Classic Bike 2009. Journalist Ben Miller got off an evening plane, the Honda NC30 was taken out of a van and we got to work. This was our final location at Sulby Bridge, when there was a last burst of light from a setting sun.

The master on the Mountain. This shot of John McGuinness for the 2012 official TT programme was made possible by shooting from a car on a road closed off for the occasion. This is the full picture, not cropped to fit the programme cover.

Above: Wonder what he was listening to? Josh Brookes prepares to ride in his first TT, the 2013 Superbike race. He would finish 10th with a fantastic last lap at 127.726mph to make him the fastest-ever newcomer.

John McGuinness - 2013 Superbike TT on the starting grid

All eyes were on McGuinness, including those of rival Guy Martin (seen over John's left shoulder) before the start of the race, which had been postponed to allow sufficient practice time. The Honda TT Legends team paid tribute to the great Joey Dunlop by repainting John's Superbike to match the Honda on which Joey took his 24th TT win at his last TT, shortly before his death in 2000. John's red leathers and yellow helmet replicated those worn by Joey in that Formula 1 race.

"That race was a little bit tough," John said, on being shown this photo. "It would have been nicer if the start hadn't been delayed. What we were doing was meant to be secret but it had been difficult to keep it under wraps. I'd been hiding in a tent, where it was hot like a greenhouse and all sorts of thoughts were going through my head. Maybe I was thinking about it too much. There was only one Joey Dunlop and the tribute was a great honour for me."

John finished third behind Michael and the third Honda rider Cameron Donald.

"I was asleep for the first two laps. I honestly can't put my finger on why – I'm only human. But it started coming together towards the end of the race and breaking the record on the last lap (131.671mph) redeemed it, so I think I did an honest job."

2014 Superstock Pit Lane

The action in the pits has its own excitement. When riders pull in to refuel, change rear tyres and clean or replace visors every split second is vital, yet the potential for panic or bungling is huge – as I know from my own Manx GP experience! Three riders have all pitted together here: Dean Harrison (furthest from camera) Conor Cummins (in the middle) and William Dunlop.

I asked William if his pit stops are panicky and he said no: the Dunlop dynasty can call on some of the most experienced pit helpers in the game.

After two close shaves with pit lane fires during the 2014 TT, the organisers have imposed tighter safety regulations, making fire-resistant clothing and headgear compulsory for riders' pit crews.

Michael Dunlop - 2013 Senior TT/St Ninian's Crossroads

Son of five-times TT winner Robert Dunlop and nephew of 26-times winner Joey, hard-charging Michael has had a phenomenal TT career since 2007, taking his 10th win in 2014. In this race he was chasing his fifth win of the meeting, but finished second to his Honda team-mate John McGuinness and had to settle for four.

Cameron Donald - 2010 Practice/Bray Hill

This remote shot is better than I could have hoped for: I didn't expect to see both wheels off the road at this point. "I never realised I was airborne this far down the hill, but maybe that's why I had to close the throttle on that lap," Cam told me. "I was probably a little off my ideal line over the crest. When all is working well you can take Bray Hill without rolling off, but if the bike gets out of shape you will need to roll it back until you get where you need to be. "You pass the grandstand at well over 170mph and if you haven't rolled off for the crest, it would have to be 180mph-plus here, in sixth gear. Bray Hill is a buzz when the bike is working with you and you can keep the throttle open. The force on your body through the dip at the bottom is huge, but you don't really notice it with all the adrenaline pumping!" Cam explained the ragged front mudguard: "We didn't have a race kit carbon fibre guard that year and the standard glassfibre one flexed under wind force and rubbed on the tyre."

Dan Kneen - 2011
Superbike/Bray Hill

It was the first lap and I was lying behind a wall. Out of my view and above the wail of an engine I heard an almighty metallic 'crack' quickly followed by spectators' screams. I looked, and saw Dan wrestling his Kawasaki in a horrifying wobble. Miraculously he didn't crash and the laid-back Manx ace described the incident to me later.

"For a split second there, I thought I was going through someone's front door. The bike had been handling badly for the whole fortnight and after I came over the rise at the top of the hill the front wheel landed and went lock-to-lock all the way down. The 'bars were trying to rip themselves out of my hands."

Did he contemplate bailing out?

"No. If you thought like that you'd be jumping off all the time! You'd only get off if you knew you had no chance of regaining control."

In 1998 Dan was the first rider to win three Manx GP races in one year. Since then he has had nine top-ten finishes in TTs including fifth in a 2010 Supersport.

Ian Lougher - 2013 Senior/Bray Hill

A remote camera shot taken at the foot of the hill on the first lap. This was supreme roads racer Ian's last TT after a record number of starts over 30 years and 10 wins. I asked him if it was an emotional occasion. "It was, but I had to concentrate on the race: you can't let mind wander. But it did hit me on my last run over the Mountain, the section I like the best. Here at Bray Hill it's like a roller coaster. You tell yourself to get on line and think about what happened last time you went down. It has been smoothed out at the bottom since I started racing. There was even a manhole right on the line years ago, when we used to race in the rain – and fog. My best and hardest race was when I beat Steve Hislop in the 1990 250cc Junior, because for me he was the greatest and fastest ever. I was at the 2014 TT but glad not to be out there, with pressure on to do a 128mph lap off the line. I had got tired and I'd lost so many friends".

John McGuinness - Senior TT 2013/Quarterbridge Road

This is the slight crest by the junction of Selbourne Drive with Quarterbridge Road just beyond Ago's leap, sometimes called Ago's 2 and a little bit faster. It's also harder to photograph, as you need a low angle to catch that important daylight under the back wheel and approaching bikes are invisible till the last second. John won this one, despite Michael Dunlop being favourite after winning the previous four solo races that year. "It was one of the highlights of my TT career," he told me. "All I needed to be was where I left off in the Superbike race with the record lap and I was in with a shout. The bike was good, the team were a million per cent and I was back in my Legends leathers. It was one of those races where I got all the apexes right, had two great pit stops and the weather conditions were perfect. Through Ago's, you just just have to go where the bike takes you, honestly. Here I'm pressing the thumb brake on the left handlebar to steady up."

Klaus Klaffenbock /Dan Sayle, John Holden /Andy Winkle - 2011 Sidecar 2/Braddan Bridge

The passengers are not only throwing their weight to the right to help keep the machines stable; they are also putting weight on the rear wheels. "If the passenger is not right on the back wheel, you get wheel-spin and lose time accelerating away," explained Klaus, known to everyone as Klaffi. He confirmed that he holds his engine flat-out on the red line from Union Mills to Greeba Castle, for just under two minutes. "But I only hold it on through Ballagarey in races," he said. "Never in practice." German driver Klaffi came to the TT in 2004 with the 2001 Sidecar world championship under his belt. He took a double win in 2010 with Manxman Dan Sayle as his passenger. He rates that double as his greatest racing achievement, even above his world title. "The mileage you do at the TT is like 12 rounds of a world championship," he said.

Luis Carreira - 2010 Practice/Braddan Bridge

Close to the action with a remote camera clamped to railings on the bridge at Braddan, with Luis's face visible through a tinted visor. Sadly the Portuguese rider, who raced at four TTs from 2009, lost his life in a crash during qualification for the 2012 Macau Grand Prix.

Opposite page: Guy Martin - 2010 Practice/Braddan Bridge, exit

An excited spectator urges Mr Martin to gives his Superbike even more throttle. Always a potential winner, backed by a huge fan base, real roads specialist Guy has racked up wins in the Southern 100, at Oliver's Mount Scarborough and in Ireland, but has yet to reach the top step on the TT podium. Made famous beyond motorcycling by his TV work, Guy had a central role in the 2011 documentary film Closer to the Edge, a worldwide hit that did much to increase interest in the TT.

John McGuinness - 2013 Senior/Union Mills

Taken with a remote camera in early-evening sunlight. The inky black background effect can only be caught for a short time in the summer months. John brushes a knee-slider on the inside kerb at this downhill right-hander. I asked for his comments.

"Some new bumps appeared in the last couple of years and I try to keep inside of them. Union Mills is not my favourite section, but it's really important. You need to get a good line through here and especially the left that follows, so you can be hard on the power early to go up the Ballahutchin Straight." Was he then flat-out all the way to Greeba? "No, I knock it back to fifth at Ballagarey. You can't go through there flat in top on a Superbike, whatever anyone else says."

Cameron Donald - 2010 Practice/Union Mills

You can see Cam's eyes fixed on the road ahead, thanks to the clear visor. He normally favours tinted visors so I asked about that. "A mid-tint is a good compromise for most conditions, but if there's a grey sky or it's late evening, even a light tint will be too dark to see clearly under the trees in a section like Glen Helen. I'm focused on one of my hundreds of reference points around the course. Most are well down the road ahead, as the farther ahead your focus is, the better. If you focus on things directly in your path, the sensation of speed can be overwhelming".

Antonio Maeso - 2013 Practice/Glen Vine

Taken on the gentle descent just beyond the Ballagarey right-hander in evening light. I showed this to Antonio, who describes what's happening:

"It helps to keep a steady wheelie going after the first change of elevation exiting 'Ballascary'. If the front wheel is on the deck as you get back on the power, bumps on the road cause uncomfortable floating or shimmies. Besides that, it's one of the most fascinating wheelies you could possibly dream of, as the speed you are travelling at here is so outrageously high. Passing a 'School Slow' sign doing a 160mph wheelie makes my devil side happy!"

Spanish rider Antonio crashed in the 2013 Superbike race sustaining a leg injury. Although forced to miss the 2014 TT, he is keen to return when he's fit enough.

Bruce Anstey - 2011 Practice/Appledene

Low sun from Braddan Bridge to Kirk Michael can be a hindrance for riders during a fine weather evening practice, but not for photographers. This shot of a well-lit bike and rider against a dark background shows why. Nine-times TT winner Bruce became the fastest ever rider in 2014, lapping at 132.298mph in the Superbike race.

Bruce Anstey - 2011 Practice/Appledene

A remote shot taken within seconds of the preceding photo, with the shadow cast by the camera visible on the right.

Spectators - 2014 Lightweight/Knock Breck Farm

Typical TT atmosphere. I've waited a long time to get this shot and had to grab it in the morning, when the sun is in the perfect position. The previous year, I'd driven the narrow back roads like a Manx Rally competitor to get here. I arrived just in time for the fourth and final lap, the only problem being that it was a three-lap race.

John Ingram - 2014 Practice/Knock Breck Farm

Taken from the wall of Knock Breck farmyard, seven miles from the start. The hospitable Harold Leece welcomes spectators onto his property, with seats, standing areas and refreshments available. Riders appear round a fast right-hander and streak past towards the Gorse Lea curve at around 160mph. John Ingram's best result in 2014 was 29th place in the Superstock race.

Marshals - 2014/Gorse Lea

Not an action shot, but there would be no racing without the all-important marshals. This group of Sector 3 volunteers I met during a practice session at the terrifyingly fast Gorse Lea section are (from left) : Paul McAuley, 'Yorkie', John Hall (seated), John Foster and Phil Holland (at back), Henry Bridson (also St John Ambulance), Brian Heap, Reg Berrie and Paddy O'Neill. Between them these guys can claim more than 75 years of TT and Manx GP attendance at Gorse Lea, while another 15-20 marshals regularly cover the stretch of road named after a property beside the Course. "It had been very much under-manned," John Foster told me. "But after the death of the New Zealand rider Stu Murdoch in 1999, Phil, Reg and I were recruited by Eric Alexander." Eric is the longest-serving marshal, whose first duties were before World War Two. He won the Spirit of the TT Award in 2014.

Previous page:

Dean Harrison - 2014 Practice/Gorse Lea

This right-hand curve is one of the fastest, scariest places I've been to. What makes this shot for me is Dean's bush baby eyes and the red tint on his face. When I showed him this photo, he confirmed that the red is reflecting off the Kawasaki's rev counter, where an LED light comes on to warn of the engine's rev limit.

"If I go through there in fifth the light will come on just before I change up," Dean told me. "Mostly I go through in sixth, so as not to damage the engine. That's about 170mph. I still haven't got Gorse Lea nailed. It has a double apex and early in practice I try to turn in too early. You need to turn in later and keep your eyes peeled for the apexes. It's all good fun!"

A TT rider since 2011, Dean has lapped at over 130mph and took his first win in the 2014 Lightweight.

Bruce Anstey - 2012 Supersport A/Glen Helen

Bruce is about to brush the grass growing on a solid roadside bank with his left shoulder. Not a man of many words, he told me that this is perfectly normal and that he uses the yielding blades of grass as the apex of this sweeping left-hander.

John McGuinness - 2012 Superstock /Glen Helen

This was John's only Superstock TT win, on a 1000cc Padgett's Honda Fireblade. "I seemed to have a mental block with Superstocks, even though I've ridden them week in and week out at British Superbike meetings. Maybe everyone else wasn't quite on form. I only drag my knee in a few places and if you look at photos, you'll see that I hang off more on the left than the right. I've got three big screws in my right hip."

William Dunlop - 2012 Supersport 1/Glen Helen

Michael Dunlop's older brother emerges from the shadows around the right-hand kink before Glen Helen's tighter main left-hander, on a 600cc Honda. William told me that this twisty and undulating section following Laurel Bank is his favourite part of the Course. He finished third in this race, his first podium result on the Mountain Course.

Opposite page:

John McGuinness - 2012 TT Zero practice/Glen Helen

A strong contrast of afternoon light and shade. This was the first year John rode the amazing Mugen Shinden electric bike, to finish second at 102.2mph. Two years later he won with a sub-20-minute lap at 117.36mph, showing how serious the Japanese team is about investing in the development of battery-powered two-wheelers.

"I have a lot of respect for those bikes and the people behind them. I reckon I can take some places faster on this than on the Superbike. It's a heavy bike, weighing 260kg, and it stays on line easier. I loved every minute of it."

Gary Johnson - 2011 Senior/Molyneux's

Gary was on his first lap when he got this scary wobble on. He was heading straight for the camera and very nearly clipped my shoulder. Always analytical, Gaz explained that changes had been made to his Honda's front suspension settings.

"I was struggling to get the forks to turn in, which meant making more input through the 'bars," he said. "As the front wheel lifts off the tarmac, the steering gets lighter and you can over-turn, then as it lands it tends to self-straighten and you get the wobble effect. I take this one flat in sixth, after giving the rear thumb brake a touch to steady up on the entry."

Yoshinari Matsushita - 2012 Practice/Handley's Corner

This was the first time I'd been at Handleys since 2005. I prefer to let a few years pass before returning to the same points. Road surfaces change and trees grow larger, or even come down in high winds, which can change a section's dynamic, light and background. My favoured angle on the outside of the course here is now a Prohibited Area but I was relatively safe high up on this wall. Sadly, popular Japanese rider 'Matsu', here on his BMW Superstock, was killed in a high-speed crash practising for the 2013 TT.

Guy Martin - 2012 Practice/Barregarrow (top)

This was the first time in over 20 years I used this particular angle and nothing has changed: the front wheels still chatter, although with their increased engine power, Superbikes now stand on their back wheels as the road drops away down the hill.

John Holden /Andy Winkle - 2010 Sidecar A/Barregarrow (top)

Sidecar action can be dramatic at the top of Barregarrow. John Holden powers through the left-hander as passenger Andy Winkle hangs out to combat forces hoisting the sidecar wheel off the road. It looks pretty frightening, but Andy thinks otherwise. " It's normal and nothing to get excited about," he told me. "The faster you are going, the more that wheel will want to lift. If you feel it coming up, you shift your weight further out. But you must always be on your guard: there could be a stone wall coming up." In this race, the crew's LCR Suzuki did not last the race, but they finished second in Sidecar B, behind the Klaffenbock/Sayle duo.

Conor Cummins - 2010 Superbike TT/Barregarrow (bottom)

The bottom of Barregarrow is one of those beyond spectacular places that I'm tempted to go back to every year, but there are too many other places I must try. Since my last visit here in 2007, a privet hedge on the right side had been ripped out, affording a previously unobtainable angle from the rear. Another change I noticed was that the fastest Superbikes now get completely airborne before slamming their fairings' bellypans into the tarmac in the dip.

Tall Manxman 'Con-rod' Cummins took an early lead in this race on his 1000cc McAdoo Kawasaki but was denied glory by a machine failure on lap five. He collected three podium results before his spectacular crash on the Verandah in 2010, caught on video and played countless times on YouTube. Conor proved he had recovered from his injuries by finishing second in the 2014 Senior, riding for the Honda Racing team.

Cameron Donald - 2010 Superbike/Barregarrow (bottom)

Shot remotely from the cottage gateway (the camera is visible in the previous photo). Over to Cam: "On the Superbike you drive down the hill in fifth, shifting back to fourth before the bottom. I stay seated, but grab the bike tightly with my knees against the fuel tank. Once the bike has bottomed-out through the dip, it's hard back on the throttle to keep it going straight. If you keep the bike straight it should all go to plan, but when things get a bit crossed up that kerb on the right approaches very quickly. It's certainly a 'white knuckle' section!

**Ryan Farquhar - 2012
Practice/Kirk Michael**

Follow the dotted line. A late
evening shot of the straight stretch
before the village, framed by foliage.

Irish rider Ryan Farquhar rides the
650cc Kawasaki on which he won
the inaugural Lightweight race for
twin-cylinder four-strokes. He was
the leading developer of this class
of machine, which has replaced the
racing two-stroke, now out of
favour.

Guy Martin - 2011 Practice TT/Douglas Road Corner

Even though you can only see one eye, Guy's face is recognisable through his clear visor as he rushes his Tyco Suzuki Superbike through the bumpy 90mph bend on the entry to Kirk Michael village.

Simon Andrews - 2012 Practice TT/Kirk Michael

I shot this from a hoist, elevated to 9m (30ft) above ground level, to get a unique view through the village, with the road's white centre line snaking off into the distance. The idea was to catch a flood of bikes charging through, but it was this shot of a lonely Simon Andrews riding through long evening shadows that worked best. This photo took on greater significance for me after Simon's untimely death following a crash at the North West 200 in May 2014.

Klaus Klaffenbock/Dan Sayle - 2011 Sidecar practice/Kirk Michael

"Shall I put the kettle on dear?" The TT combines the extreme and dangerous with the homely and everyday. Race winner Klaus Klaffenbock and passenger Dan Sayle streak past the front doors of Main Road, Kirk Michael village on their 140mph Honda outfit.

Greg Lambert/Jason Slous - 2010 Sidecar 2/Kirk Michael

Passenger Slous tucks away out of the draught beside the rear wheel as driver Lambert powers towards the end of the village. Whitehouse Park across the road on this gentle left-left sweep has become a paid-for spectating spot in recent years. Greg took third place in the Sidecar TT in 1999 and 2003. Isle of Man-based Jason passengered for him in the 2010 TT, when still in his teens.

Dean Harrison - 2014 Lightweight (winner)/Kirk Michael

I go out scouting for new angles in the weeks before the TT, which can mean spending a lot of time in one place. I found this position by spending a couple of hours walking up and down through Kirk Michael village one quiet evening. Later on, I was greeted by a police patrol scrambled from Peel, reacting to a phone call reporting 'a shabby unshaven man acting suspiciously'. "I am flat-out in sixth here on the Lightweight, but not on the Superbike," Dean told me. "I quite like Kirk Michael, where you're always having to look ahead as far as you can to be sure where the road goes."

Bruce Anstey - 2012 Practice/Rhencullen

A remote shot with the camera fixed on a tripod and manually pre-focused, with me at a safe distance. The white houses out of focus behind Bruce's shoulder are where TV footage showed him within millimetres of leaving the road on his 132mph record lap in the 2014 Superbike race. When I asked him about that, Bruce smiled, shrugged his shoulders and said it was his normal line. He thought the lap 'felt quick' but the record came as a surprise to him, which is what top Mountain Course riders have often said.

Previous page:

Josh Brookes - 2014 Supersport 2/Rhencullen

One giant leap...I asked Josh if he would be on the same line as this on his Superbike.

"The line is not so different," he explained. "It's the body position and the angle of the bike at the point of take-off that's important. Once you know it and do it right, you gain confidence and get quicker and quicker, resulting in more time in the air. It's the same with the Superbike but more difficult because of the torque steer effect from the power."

Josh told me he prefers riding the 1000cc Superbike to the 600cc Supersport at the TT. Interesting, as riders often say they find the less powerful and lighter Supersport more enjoyable. Did he have any big scares in his debut year?

"No, I'm pleased to say, although in this race a strong wind pushed me wide on the exit to the Verandah and I went on the grass for a few metres. I lost some time, but it wasn't scary."

Originally from Australia, Josh came to the TT in 2013 having already made a name on short circuits. He lived up to expectations by being the fastest-ever newcomer, lapping at 127.726mph in the Superbike race.

Michael Dunlop - 2014 Senior (winner)/Bishops Court

Head down and front wheel up, on the factory-backed BMW HP4. Dunlop gave the German marque a dream result on the 75th anniversary of its last Senior win, by Georg Meier in 1939.

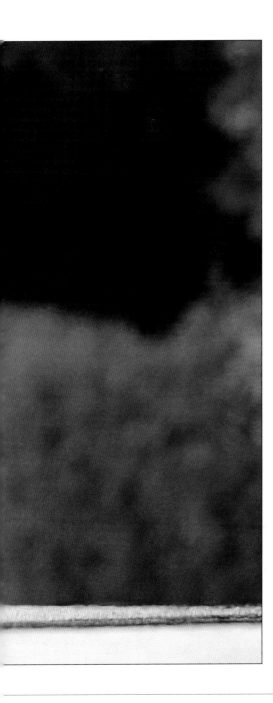

Ian Hutchinson - 2010 Superstock (winner)/near Orrisdale Road North

On his sensational 130mph Superstock record last lap with a light fuel load, Hutchy is banked over and momentarily fully airborne at around 180mph.

This is one of the corners where spectating has been prohibited in recent years. The verges here used to be crammed with hardcore adrenaline junkies, shoulder to shoulder between the trees, oooh-ing and aah-ing as front wheels twisted and shook over the slight crest.

Ian had an incredible year in 2010, winning all five solo races on Padgett Hondas. In this race, he narrowly grabbed victory over Ryan Farquhar on the thrilling final lap.

John McGuinness - 2010 Practice/Ballaugh Bridge

Photos of the Ballaugh jump, an iconic TT image since time immemorial, are mostly shot from the landing side of the hump-backed bridge. I like to shoot from various angles, to get something different.

John said he'd tried various techniques here but it's always hit and miss and hard to be consistent.

"It's first gear on the Superbike I'm riding here, at 40-50mph and second on the Stocker or Supersport. I don't really like Ballaugh. I ride off-road a lot, but road racers don't feel great up in the air."

Josh Brookes - 2014 Supersport 1/Ballaugh

The bike doesn't always have to be in the middle of the frame. This is Josh Brookes with his wheels out of line as he accelerates his 600cc Milwaukee Yamaha through Ballaugh village, creating a heat haze.

Gary Johnson - 2013 Practice TT/Ballaugh

Here Gary is on the MV Agusta 675 Supersport which, he told me, is the best sounding bike he's ridden in the TT.

"Unfortunately the MV was under-developed and slow at that time. I got ninth in the second Supersport but I don't feel I was riding bad. Don't get me wrong, it's a decent bike that's capable of winning races, as was shown when it won a world Supersport race this year (2014)."

Gary told me he hadn't seen the cameras being dangled from the roof of the bus shelter.

Gary Johnson - 2014 Supersport 1/Ballacrye

A remote shot taken by my ace assistant Christine (so good I married her).

Meticulously planned remote shots don't always come off - you have to be prepared for disappointment. But when they do work, they can knock everything else out the window. I had positioned the camera too close to the jump, so had four laps of shots with the front wheel or the rider's helmet out of frame. All except one on a weird line: winner Gary Johnson on his 675cc Triumph.

"I had heard that the jump is smaller on the left side of the road but on the Superbike I struggled to get over that way. I thought I'd try it with the Supersport, which is travelling slower and you can turn a bit tighter. It worked, I was quite happy with it. When you leave the ground you're in sixth and the engine's bogging down when you land, so the more you can stay on the road the better."

Michael Dunlop - 2013 Practice/Quarry Bends

The first rider to appear in this session, Michael took an exceptionally tight line on his Honda and kicked up a cloud of dust that made spectators gasp. This was the extra Saturday practice arranged because bad weather had badly disrupted the previous scheduled sessions. It meant moving the Superbike race from Saturday to Sunday.

Bruce Anstey - 2013 Practice/Quarry Bends

This was taken at 1/60th of a second, usually too slow a shutter speed unless the road surface is super smooth. With panning shots like this, modern high pixel-number cameras show up the slightest camera shake more than the dear old film type. But an advantage of digital is that you can check your results immediately.

Next page:

Olie Linsdell - 2013 Supersport/Ginger Hall pub

You can drink in the bar of the Ginger Hall and still have a view of the left-hand bend outside. Olie finished 18th in this race, took sixth in the 2013 Lightweight on a Italian Paton and later that year won the inaugural 500cc Classic TT race on a Paton.

The ghostly image in the upper window frame is an old photo of 1960 Sidecar TT winner Helmut Fath.

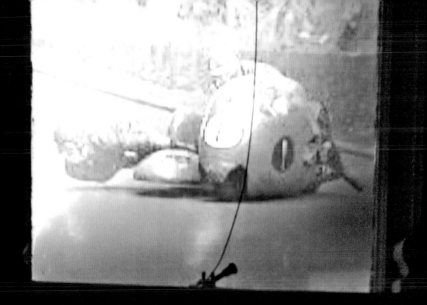

2013 - TT Zero Practice/Ginger Hall pub

Yes, I did partake of a pint while I was in here. From this position I could have poured it myself.

William Dunlop - 2013 Superstock/Ginger Hall

Looking across to the pub from the exit of the left-hander it overlooks, which clearly holds no fear for Dunlop, well banked over and headed for ninth place in this race on his 1000cc Yamaha. Known for great rides on 250cc bikes, he told me he prefers racing the lighter 600cc machines at the TT. But William showed he was up for serious big bike action by taking an early lead in the 2014 Senior. Unfortunately he crashed heavily on the Mountain on his third lap, miraculously escaping with broken bones in his leg.

**John McGuinness - 2013 Supersport Race 2/
Lezayre Conker Fields**

"This is one of the roughest sections on the track, you hold your breath a bit through here," John told me. "The approach is completely blind and all the bikes I've ridden except the 125s wheelie here. On the 600cc Supersport, you're on full gas all the way from the previous Glentramman left-hander. It's really unpredictable - you never know how big the wheelie will be. Sometimes you'll make a smooth landing and it looks like you really know what you are doing, or it may get a bit wobbly."

Michael Dunlop - 2013 Supersport 2/Lezayre Conker Fields

This was the first time I'd been here since a misty 5am practice back in 1989, when the only people present were myself and an on-duty policeman. These days this stretch is packed, made infamous by ITV4's superb coverage with cameraman Bob Blockley's hi-motion 800 frames-per-second footage. What I wanted to show was not just another bike doing a wheelie, but the numbers of spectators that flock here.

It was especially busy on this flaming hot June day with hundreds of spectators around, all seemingly equipped with video capture smart phones, eager to emulate Bob, on tippy toes with arms stretched out - right in the way of my shot. There's nothing you can do, but wait till the next lap and maybe the next after that. So I implemented Plan B by climbing a tree to get an angle I'd worked out weeks earlier. Good job the Peel Police didn't see me.

Next page:

Dave Molyneux/Patrick Farrance - 2012 Sidecar 2 (winners)/Gooseneck

It's usual to focus on the tight uphill right-hander that the Gooseneck gets its name from, but I like this shot with spectators beyond the corner, where Dave is accelerating hard away up the Mountain and Patrick is in position for the long leftward sweep ahead.

Local driver and outfit constructor Moly won both Sidecar races in 2012, taking his running total of wins to 16 and making him the first competitor to win TT races powered by all four of the leading Japanese makes, Yamaha, Honda, Suzuki and Kawasaki, in that order. Moly notched up his 17th victory in 2014.

Young fans - 2013 Sidecar practice/near 26th Milestone

I shouted across the road to these cheeky-looking lads from Ramsey that if they would put their mobile phones away, they could be in the photo. I told them not to look at the camera – mistake! Seconds later they had their phones out again.

Russ Mountford - 2014 Practice/near Guthrie Memorial

Russ told me he'd be flat-out in fourth gear at around 120mph here on this Superstock Kawasaki.

"I really like the Mountain section," he said. "My favourite part used to be from Handley's to Kirk Michael but now I can't wait to get up here. You need to scratch short circuit-style to make up time. It's very open with a lot less markers than the lower sections: I use marshal's boxes and the paint on the road as mine. On the Mountain Mile, I'm watching for the white walls at the end of the straight and exiting the Verandah you can see riders ahead and judge whether you are catching them up."

Second in the 2007 Newcomers Manx GP, Russ Mountford raced in the TT from 2009 and after missing 2010 due to injury, competed every year since. His best result was fifth in the 2012 Lightweight.

Previous page:

William Dunlop - 2014 practice /Guthrie Memorial

A remote camera caught this shot of William through the sharp right-hander, where a tight line has to be taken because of an off-camber exit can draw the bike off-line approaching the left-hander that follows.

Keith Amor - 2011 Practice/33rd Milestone

Another shot taken with a remote camera, on the three fast kinks taken in one between Windy Corner and Keppel Gate. It makes Keith look as though he going quite slowly here, although the front wheel is only just in contact with the road. I asked him if it felt as slow as it looks.

"No, it feels really fast," he said. "In fact, it's frightening! You come in flat in fifth on the rev limiter and the big bike doesn't like turning, it tries to sit up all the while. I'm in gear and the back wheel is spinning up, which can help a bit to help make the bike steer. Sticking my knee out may help a little bit, too, but nota great deal."

Scot Keith Amor, here on a Honda TT Legends team Superbike quickly took to the TT after his 2007 debut, reaching the podium in 2009 and taking second place in a 2011 Supersport. He missed two years but returned in 2014.

John McGuinness - 2014 Practice/Keppel Gate

Manx evenings are long in early summer: this was taken shortly after 9pm under a cloudless sky. The dry stone walls glowed yellow for a short time then fell into shadow as the low sun dipped behind Slieu Ruy. It was a difficult year for him, nursing a wrist injury, so his win and shattering 117mph lap on the Mugen electric bike must have been rewarding.

Next page:

Dave Hewson - 2011 Supersport 2/Kate's Cottage

Kate's Cottage on the Mountain descent appears in countless photos, but this long shot looking down, with the Clypse reservoir in the background, offers an unusual view. A competitor since 2007, stylish rider Dave Hewson finished 28th in this race on his Yamaha.

Keith Amor - 2010 Senior/Hilberry

Keith lines up for the right-hand curve at around 160mph on the HM Plant Honda Superbike originally allotted to Steve Plater, a non-starter after being injured at the North West 200. Keith told me that he has sometimes crossed the solid white the line, making spectators shrink back, but it could make the bike unstable.

"It's fast, fast, fast and I've seen people jumping out of the way when I go down there," he said.

I asked Keith if there are some places where he's on the absolute limit.

"You have to be on the absolute limit at every corner if you want to win. But you treat each single corner with respect; if you don't, it'll bite you and you'll end up in hospital – at best."

Opposite page:

Ian Hutchinson - 2010 Senior/Finish line

Exultant at taking his record-breaking fifth win, Ian stands on the footrests with his hands up as he slows after taking the flag. I sat in on an interview he gave to John Hogan of Superbike magazine and noted these comments, reproduced here with John's permission.

"This is the only race of the five I won, where I let myself celebrate over the line...with all the other races that week I would finish them, and immediately start the build-up for the next race.

"The team want you to win each race as it comes along but all the pressure is my own. There was less pressure in this race than any other."

Clive Padgett/Ian Hutchinson - 2010 Senior/winner's enclosure

"Before the start I just told him to enjoy himself, which is what I always say to riders," Clive recalled. "When he came in after winning I just said 'Flipping incredible!' - or I may have used slightly stronger language."

Clive was so pleased with Hutchy that he gave him a big kiss on the cheek.

FRIENDS IN THE SOUTH

Although similar to the TT in that it is run over a public roads course, the Southern 100 differs from the 'big un' in many ways. The Billown circuit is much shorter than the Mountain Course, at 4.25 Miles, the races for solos and sidecars have massed starts and the friendly 'Southern' has the air of a well-kept secret, as it receives little media coverage in the UK or beyond.

First staged in 1956 by the Isle of Man's enterprising Southern MCC, the meeting was originally built around a 100-mile feature race and has been held on the Billown course near Castletown annually ever since. Its early July date used to coincide with the Island's busy period for summer tourism and its close proximity to Ronaldsway Airport is handy. Now organised by the Southern 100 MCC and staged under a National permit, the Southern attracts riders from Ireland's lively road racing scene where similar circuits are in use, as well as some of the top TT road racers, budding local riders and a few overseas visitors.

Roughly rectangular in shape, Billown must be one of the least-changed racing circuits in the world, since only the slightest alterations have been made to the roads since the 1950s. It benefits from being low-lying and so not affected by mountain fog. The circuit is narrow in places, with the sharpest bends at the four corners of the rectangle, two being virtually hairpins. There is a long, slightly downhill, straight in addition to the fairly straight Castletown By-pass section where the startline is located. At the Billown Dip left-hander, roughly at the halfway point, the road plunges into the dark under trees. This fearsome section is known to riders as the Black Hole or the Bomb Hole. All the traditional real roads perils apply, like pavement kerbs, stone walls, telephone poles and

barbed wire. Close racing on big 1000cc Superbikes on these roads seems insane, but top contenders like Dean Harrison and Guy Martin can average 114mph for a lap.

In recent decades, additional meetings have joined the Southern 100 at Billown. The Pre-TT races for classic machines is in late May, coinciding with the start of TT fortnight, while a Post-TT event is usually held on the day after the TT's Friday finale.

With a friendly atmosphere and excellent spectating, Billown offers plenty of scope for creative photography, as is demonstrated by the selection of Dave Collister's Billown work that follows.

Riders are shown the one-minute warning board before a start at the 1989 Southern 100 meeting.

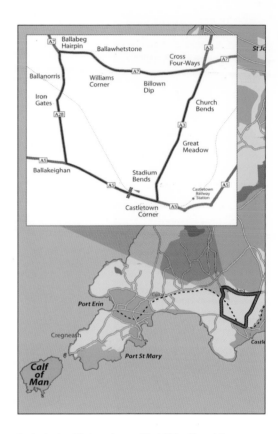

Guy Martin leads Michael Dunlop out of Billown Dip in the 2013 Southern 100 Championship Race. Many agree that the 'bomb hole' is one of the scariest places to spectate on any road circuit.

1994 - Start

Go, go, go! The flag drops on an evening Senior Founders Race, with Derek Young (4), Jason Griffiths (1), Chris Day (5), Simon Beck (2), Tim Poole (9), Joey Dunlop (3), Gary Radcliffe (7) and Alan Warner (35) prominent.

Ballakeighan 1989

A practice shot at the first corner on the circuit. Richard Coates leads David Madsen-Mygdal

Next Page: **Iron Gate Bridge 1990**

Dave Leach's bike wheelies over a hump that has been smoothed since this was taken

Joey's Gate - 2005

Guy Martin passes a farm gateway left open during practice and racing as an escape route. It was named after Joey Dunlop since he made use of it in a 1979 1300cc race, when his steering damper broke.

Joey's Gate - 2008

Joey's nephew Michael Dunlop wheelies close to the wall on a 250cc Honda two-stroke.

Ballabeg - 1999

Tim Poole leads New Zealander Blair Degerholm and Adrian Archibald round the 60-degree right-turn in Ballabeg village.

Right: **Ballawhetstone - 1998**

Simon Beck banks through the leftward kink on his 750 Kawasaki, with Steve Ellis behind. One of the best and most popular road racers, 'Big Simon' died after crashing in practice for the 1999 TT.

Previous page:

Ballawhetstone Farm - 1998

Rural peace. Seamus Elliott zips past the gateway as Jimmy looks out from his stable door.

Opposite page:

Billown Dip - 2011

Holding the LCR Honda outfit flat-out, Klaus Klaffenbock takes passenger Daniel Sayle close to the wall through the 'bomb hole'. Klaffi said he didn't recall this and was quite shocked when he saw the photo.

"Daniel didn't say anything after the race," he told me. "When he saw this, he just said 'it was the same on every lap'."

Billown Dip - 2011

Looking down on Ryan Farquhar as he accelerates away from the shaded dip.

Next page:

Cross Fourways (approach) - 1997

Owen McNally (18), Robert Dunlop (8), Ian Lougher (7), Gavin Lee (16), Joey Dunlop (3) John McCullough (41) and others head for the acute right-hard turn at the crossroads. The hill in the far background is Bradda Head, overlooking Port Erin bay.

Previous page right:

Cross Fourways (approach) - 2012

Jamie Hamilton, Ryan Farquhar, Chris Palmer and Russ Mountford battle for the lead in the 250cc two-stroke/650cc four-stroke race. This first lap made the cattle stampede, all except a black one which was either enjoying the race or had got caught on the barbed wire fence!

Cross Fourways - 2012

The leading bunch comes streaming round the corner on the first lap of a 600 Supersport race. Conor Cummins leads Michael Dunlop, Jamie Coward, Ian Lougher and Ivan Lintin.

Left:

Church Bends - 2013

A 400cc Support race shot from well inside the grounds of Malew Church.

Below:

Church Bends - 1997

Gavin Lee (Yamaha) leads Joey Dunlop (Honda) in a 250cc race.

Castletown Corner 2009

Not the Southern 100 but the 250cc Lightweight TT, moved to Billown for its final years from 2008 to 2010. Ian Lougher, eventual winner averaging 100mph, leads Roy Richardson into the right-hander before the start-finish straight.

Next page:

Finish line 1994

Joey Dunlop takes the flag on his Honda RC45 to win the Senior Solo Founders Race in the warm glow of a Manx sunset. Joey won 31 Southern 100 races.

John McGuinness 2013 Senior/Grandstand

A euphoric McGuinness after his 20th TT win. This all happened spontaneously and when John lay down I nipped up onto the winners' podium to get my own angle (and to avoid the barging and elbowing among other photographers). Luckily someone shouted at John, who looked towards me and gave a thumbs up.

John is hugely popular, but unaffected by his outstanding TT success. I have seen him signing autographs and posing for photos with fans for half an hour following a hard six-lap race.